II

CHESTER COUNTY LIBRARY
235 WEST MARKET STREET
WEST CHESTER, PA. 19380

Telephone: 696-8960

THE PIT and OTHER POEMS

THE
PIT and
OTHER
POEMS

Lucien Stryk

THE **SWALLOW PRESS** INC.

CHICAGO

Copyright © 1969 by Lucien Stryk
All rights reserved
Printed in the United States of America
Published by
The Swallow Press Incorporated
1139 South Wabash Avenue
Chicago, Illinois 60605

LIBRARY OF CONGRESS CATALOG CARD NUMBER 74-75738

ACKNOWLEDGMENTS: Antioch Review, Carolina Quarterly, Chicago Review, Chicago Tribune, Choice, December, Envoi, Epoch, Fiddlehead, Forum, Guns & Butter, Impetus, The Japanese Image (Orient/West, Inc.), Jeopardy, The Listener, Literary Review, Literature East & West, Massachusetts Review, Midwest, New Mexico Quarterly, The New York Times, Omnibus, Parnassus, Poetry and Audience, Poetry Bag, Quartet, Saturday Review, Shenandoah, The Sixties, Spectrum, Stained the Water Clear (Reed College), Today, Tri-Quarterly, Voices, Volume 63, Western Humanities Review.

"The Peach," "Horse," "Quails," "Stitches," "Fish" by Shinkichi Takahashi, translated by Lucien Stryk, copyright © 1965 by Lucien Stryk. From the book, ZEN: Poems, Prayers, Sermons, Anecdotes, Interviews by Lucien Stryk and Takashi Ikemoto. Reprinted by permission of Doubleday & Co., Inc.

"The Pit," the Isaac Rosenbaum Poetry Award poem for 1964, reprinted by permission of Voices Publishing Co.

for Dan and Lydia

contents

‖ OF BEAST AND MAN

This slowly drifting cloud is pitiful;
What dreamwalkers men become.
Awakened, I hear the one true thing—
Black rain on the roof of Fukakusa Temple.

—Dogen

I

THE PAPER HOUSE

OEUVRE

Will it ever be finished, this house
    Of paper
I began to raise when I was seventeen?

Others scramble from foundations far less firm.
    Seasons of
Pondering, name by name, the past's magnificent,

A squandering. Surely I might have lived.
    Spitefully
Watching as rivals stole the girls, got the jobs,

Won the laurels, the misery seeped in,
    Tinting the
Windows, darkening the fairest day.

But how should I have known, a house to please
    Need not be
Outlandish? And that searching everywhere

The fresh, the rare, prowling the gaudier
    Capitals,
Something of each would rub off, deface.

Well, we build where and as we can. There are
    Days when I
Am troubled by an image of the house,

Laden, rootless, like a tinseled tree,
    Suddenly
Torn to a thousand scribbled leaves and borne off

By the wind, then to be gathered and patched
    Whole again,
Or of the thing going up in smoke

And I, the paper dreamer, wide awake.

3

TO A JAPANESE POET

You stood frozen there,
One hand gripping my arm,
In the other your lunchbasket,
And when I turned
To look into your face,
It was like witnessing a birth.

When the poem came,
Your fingers loosened and you
Spoke the dozen words as if
Directing one who'd
Lost his way upon
A mountain path, the night descending.

Finally we went to join
The others, but you were not the same.
All that brilliant autumn day
You avoided me
As if I'd surprised you
In some intimacy, as if my being

Near had suddenly
Cut us off. Later, when I mentioned
A hurt no memory of scarlet leaves
Could ease, you laughed
And said, "Why should you
Have felt badly? We had an enjoyable outing."

4

ZEN: THE ROCKS OF SESSHU
(Joei Temple Garden, Yamaguchi)

I

What do they think of
   Where they lean
Like ponderous heads, the rocks?—

In prankish spring, ducks
   Joggling here
And there, brushing tails,

Like silly thoughts shared,
   Passed from head
To head? When, gong quavering

About a ripened sky, we
   Up and go,
Do they waken from a dream of flesh?

II

In the Three Whites of
    Hokusai—
Fuji, the snow, the crane—

What startles is the black: in
    The outline
Of the mountain, the branch-tips

Piercing the snow, the quills of
    The crane's wing:
Meaning impermanence.

Here, in stainless air, the
    Artist's name
Blazes like a crow.

6

III

Distance between the rocks,
   Half the day
In shadow, is the distance

Between man who thinks
   And the man
Who thinks he thinks: wait.

Like a brain, the garden,
   Thinking when
It is thought. Otherwise

A stony jumble, merely that,
   Laid down there
To stud our emptiness.

IV

Who calls her butterfly
   Would elsewhere
Pardon the snake its fangs:

In the stony garden
   Where she flits
Are sides so sharp, merely

To look gives pain. Only
   The tourist,
Kodak aimed and ready for

The blast, ship pointing for the
   Getaway,
Dare raise that parasol.

8

V

To rid the grass of weed, to get
   The whole root,
Thick, tangled, takes a strong mind

And desire—to make clean, make pure.
   The weed, tough
As the rock it leaps against,

Unless plucked to the last
   Live fiber
Will plunge up through dark again.

The weed also has the desire
   To make clean,
Make pure, there against the rock.

9

VI

It is joy that lifts those pigeons to
   Stitch the clouds
With circling, light flashing from underwings.

Scorning our crumbs, tossed carefully
   To corners
Of the garden, beyond the rocks,

They rose as if summoned from
   The futile
Groveling our love subjects them to.

Clear the mind! Empty it of all that
   Fixes you,
Makes every act a pecking at the crumb.

10

VII

Firmness is all: that mountain beyond the
    Garden path,
Watch how against its tawny slope

The candled boughs expire. Follow
    The slope where
Spearheads shake against the clouds

And dizzy the pigeons circling on the wind.
    Then observe
Where no bigger than a cragstone

The climber pulls himself aloft,
    As by the
Very guts: firmness is all.

VIII

Pierced through by birdsong, stone by stone
   The garden
Gathered light. Darkness, hauled by ropes

Of sun, entered roof and bough. Raised from
   The temple
Floor where, stiff since cockcrow,

Blown round like Buddha on the lotus,
   He began
To write. How against that shimmering,

On paper frail as dawn, make poems?
   Firm again,
He waited for the rocks to split.

THE PEACH
(after Shinkichi Takahashi)

A little girl under a peach tree,
Whose blossoms fall into the entrails
Of the earth.

There you stand, but a mountain may be there
Instead; it is not unlikely that the earth
May be yourself.

You step against a plate of iron and half
Your face is turned to iron. I will smash
Flesh and bone

And suck the cracked peach. She went up the mountain
To hide her breasts in the snowy ravine.
Women's legs

Are more or less alike. The leaves of the peach tree
Stretch across the sea to the end of
The continent.

The sea was at the little girl's beck and call.
I will cross the sea like a hairy
Caterpillar

And catch the odor of your body.

13

HORSE
(after Shinkichi Takahashi)

Young girls bloom like flowers.
Unharnessed, a horse trots
Round its driver who
Grasps it by a rope.

Far off a horse is going round and round
In a square plot.

Not miserable, not cheerful either,
The bay horse is prancing,
Shaking its head, throwing up its legs
By turn: it is not running.

But there are no spectators
In what looks like an amphitheater.

White cherry blossoms fall like snowflakes
In the wind. All at once,
Houses, people vanish, into silence.
Nothing moves. Streetcars, buses, are held back
Silently. Quiet, everything.
All visible things become this nothingness.

The horse's bones—beautiful in their gray sheen.

A horse is going round and round,
Dancing now, with *joie de vivre*,
Under the cliff of death.

QUAILS
(after Shinkichi Takahashi)

It is the grass that moves, not the quails.
Weary of embraces, she thought of
Committing her body to the flame.

When I shut my eyes, I hear far and wide
The air of the Ice Age stirring.
When I open them, a rocket passes over a meteor.

A quail's egg is complete in itself,
Leaving not room enough for a dagger's point.
All the phenomena in the universe: myself.

Quails are supported by the universe
(I wonder if that means subsisting by God).
A quail has seized God by the neck

With its black bill, because there is no
God greater than a quail.
(Peter, Christ, Judas: a quail.)

A quail's egg: idle philosophy in solution.
(There is no wife better than a quail.)
I dropped a quail's egg into a cup for buckwheat noodles,

And made havoc of the Democratic Constitution.
Split chopsticks stuck in the back, a quail husband
Will deliver dishes on a bicycle, anywhere.

The light yellow legs go up the hill of Golgotha.
Those quails who stood on the rock, became the rock!
The nightfall is quiet, but inside the congealed exuviae

Numberless insects zigzag, on parade.

STITCHES
(after *Shinkichi Takahashi*)

My wife is always knitting, knitting:
Not that I watch her,
Not that I know what she thinks.

(Awake till dawn
I drowned in your eyes—
I must be dead:
Perhaps it's the mind that stirs.)

With that bamboo needle
She knits all space, piece by piece,
Hastily hauling time in.

Brass-cold, exhausted,
She drops into bed and,
Breathing calmly, falls asleep.

Her dream must be deepening,
Her knitting coming loose.

16

FISH
(after *Shinkichi Takahashi*)

I hold a newspaper, reading.
Suddenly my hands become cow ears,
Then turn into Pusan, the South Korean port.

Lying on a mat
Spread on the bankside stones,
I fell asleep.
But a willow leaf, breeze-stirred,
Brushed my ear.
I remained just as I was,
Near the murmurous water.

When young there was a girl
Who became a fish for me.
Whenever I wanted fish
Broiled in salt, I'd summon her.
She'd get down on her stomach
To be sun-cooked on the stones.
And she was always ready!

Alas, she no longer comes to me.
An old benighted drake,
I hobble homeward.
But look, my drake feet become horse hoofs!
Now they drop off
And, stretching marvelously,
Become the tracks of the Tokaido Railway Line.

17

THE QUAKE

Alone in that paper house
We laughed when the bed
Heaved twice then threw
Us to the floor. When all

Was calm again, you said
It took an earthquake
To untwine us. Then I
Stopped your shaking

With my mouth. Together
In this place of brick,
Held firm as fruits
Upon a sculptured bough,

Our loving is more safe.
Then why should dream
Return us to that fragile
Shelf of land? And why,

Our bodies twined upon
This couch of stone,
Should we be listening,
Like dead sinners, for the quake?

18

H. S. WITH NOH MASK

Unpacking again, tired, fearing
    Another drought,
You plunge an arm into the trunk

And, holding the mask against your
    Face, stand before
The mirror searching the self

I made you leave behind: dark hair
    Flowing with its
Three loose strands, eyes burning back

To where you always are, cheeks
    Like sides of tusks
And there, through parted lips

The squares of blackened teeth which
    Alone are strange.
How naturally you pose in time

Back here in Chicago
    Where tomorrow,
Noh mask hung upon the wall,

You must try to make a life.

19

RETURN TO DEKALB

Expecting no miracle, we found none:
One retarred blacktop, another supermart,
    The sum of change—

Apart from the waiting neighbors, in which
Plentiful loss of hair and swollen girth,
    Those additions

To a catalogue of woes, came as small
Surprise. We were the lucky travelers
    Come back to plan

A further flight, happy to learn that none
Remembered an earthquake in Persia or
    Rioting in Greece.

Suddenly sick of so much reality,
We climbed the long-worn staircase to the
    Bedroom, and found

What each had thought was shaken off—Time
Rose stinking from the mattress, perched, a
    Raven, on the sill.

THE ANNIVERSARY

The sun rising,
   The sun setting,
Takes no more beauty
   On than yours
Whom the years have
   Carried like a vessel
Across the grinding seas.

I ride you like
   A Sinbad, seeking
What I have but
   Cannot find until
The Roc lies plucked
   And bleeding on
The shore all sailors curse.

O love, this ten years'
   Voyage in your arms
Has taught me nothing
   That I did not know
When, sighting you, I swam
   To board the one fair ship
Among the blistered prows.

VOYAGER

And how he pities the man with an arm
About the girl who, like a tug, guides
Him through the high sea of aloneness,
Certain to toss him on the nearest shore,

Should another beckon. Forever solitary,
How he feels for those that go, two by two,
In the illusion of togetherness.
Watching outside the Greyhound Station

For the carriage that will take him anywhere,
He is part of all: in every city
Painted mouths are pouting to be bruised,
A thousand sheets, stretching like a snowfield,

Await the restless imprint of his limbs.
The voyager can cherish the heart fulfilled
For its illusion of fulfillment
As he moves in the dream of arrival.

LOVER

Always the exile
Learning a strange landscape,
    Unsure

Of self, certain only
Of the moon, despite her
    New face

And the memory,
Vaguely troubling as
    Her light,

Of promises in
A country true
    As this.

ÉTUDE

I was cycling by the river, back and forth,
    Umbrella up against the
        Rain and blossoms.

It was very quiet, I thought of Woolworth
    Globes you shake up snowstorms in.
        Washed light slanted

Through the cherry trees, and in a flimsy house
    Some youngster practiced Chopin.
        I was moving

With the current, wheels squishing as the music
    Rose into the trees, then stopped,
        And from the house

Came someone wearing too much powder, raincape
    Orchid in the light. Middle-aged,
        The sort you pass

In hundreds everyday and scarcely notice,
    The Chopin she had sent
        Up to those boughs,

Petals spinning free, gave her grace no waters
    Would reflect, but I might
        Long remember.

24

THAT WOMAN THERE

Will she ever go away, that woman there?
Every night she stands with arms upraised,
High throat twisting in the streetlamp's noose.

One by one they come, the wild beseechers—
Merchants, students, thieves, he who squats before,
Shaking a bouquet of dollars at her knees.

O she is cruel to keep them, eyes plucking
At these half-drawn blinds. What does she hope
To offer, fingers spread, sharp heels grinding?

Must she be told that He has left for good?

25

SONG FOR ONE

After the wedding,
The flung rice and boots,
   The guests like fountains
Gushing on the lawn
   (Her arms around him
   Like a noose)
It was good to get out of town,
   Lay her down
  In the dark of a room
He would never see again.

After the honeymoon,
Niagara and the Empire State,
   The coins and tokens
Pelting from his purse
   (Her body like a doe
   Lashed to a hood)
It was sad to get back to town,
   Lay her down
  In the dark of a room
He had hated from the start.

THE LOCUSTS

Whirring from the desert, so dense
      We thought the sand
Was heaving to engulf us,

The locusts raised a wind. Sunlight
      Scarcely filtered
Through, then, sudden decimator,

The car made paste-and-membrane
      Of their swarming,
Trophied where a hundred spanning

Wings and wrenched sky-hopping legs
      Had clung. We moved
Through famished miles, blind, remembered

Plagues as thick and foul about us.
      Reaching town, I
Hosed the car down for a day,

Then sold it. Today whenever
      I think of her,
Locusts, locusts, break around me.

OBJET d'ART

The copper bowl I keep
    Tobacco
In is thick with nightingales

And roses, up to the
    Minaret
Its lid, incised so-so.

I no longer smoke in
    Company,
It seems indecent:

Reminded by those birds
    And flowers
Of a botched renown,

A Persian I once
    Had for tea
Turned from it and wept.

SNOWS

I

All night thick flakes have fallen,
The street below lies smothered
        With the past.
One remembers other snows
        (Images
In snapshots framed by the chill
Edge), ablaze before the thaw.

II

Disburdenment is what mind seeks
Above all other riches,
        Disburdenment
Of little griefs gathered like drifts
Into each corner. I think of
        This as, shovel
Arcing wide, breath peopling the air,
I hurl slosh like diamonds at
        A snout of sun.

29

TREES

I

For five years now
I've caught you
At your tricks,

Marveling as you've
Stirred after the brown
Death, the white.

Envious, I watch
You where the
Words don't come—

Remembering
A quick flame,
The settling of ash.

II

All day the powersaws whir,
Sick trees come down, festering
    The walk with limbs.

The old street stretches to cornfields
Like an amputee. Above the
    Rip-tooth clamor

Of a long-awaited spring,
Birds wheel like exiles in
    A time of war.

IMAGE

The house
Huge ugly plant
Peeling rotting
Around us
Making dark dark
Draining
Cutting off
It will see
Our end
Its floorboards
Sinking
To our dead weight

MEMO TO THE BUILDER

. . . and then
After the roof goes up
Remember to lay the eave trough
Wide and deep. A run
For squirrels and a river
For my birds. You know, I'd rather

You made the trough
So, than have the rooftop
Tarred and shingled. Keep
It in mind, the trough.
Also I'm not so sure of glass
In every window. But let that pass.

Still—and there are
Reasons enough, believe me—
It would please no end to be
In and out together.
And how it would thrill me should a bird,
Learning our secret, make a whir-

ring thoroughfare
Of a room or two.
Forget the weather. To
Have the wild, the rare
Not only happen, mind, but
Be the normal is exactly what

I'm after. Now
You know. Perhaps you
Think I've made your job too
Light? Good. Throw
Caution to the beams. Build me a home
The living day can enter, not a tomb.

32

II
OF BEAST AND MAN

CROW

He is made giddy by the sun,
And is stupid enough to race
Its rise and fall, so that at dawn

One spots him lumbering across the
Winter sky, then perched like a heart
Within the skeletal tree.

Wherever he goes he carries
His stomach like a weapon,
And the small bird hungering flies

In his wake, hoping for a crumb
As the foul beak chews and caws
Together and the black wings climb.

Devourer of acres, he drops
On the puny scarecrow and plants
Tomorrow's morsel between the flaps

Of its straw-stuck coat. Nothing
Frightens him, the hawk will whirl
From what he swoops for, this king

Of field and fat metropolis.
And already taken over
From the eagle, he must replace

That ancient master of the sky
On escutcheon and dollar.
In this usurpation he

Most resembles us: image of
Our gutty need and power, he
Merits all our rubbish and our love.

CORMORANT

Men speak lightly of frustration,
As if they'd invented it.

As if like the cormorant
Of Gifu, thick leg roped, a ring

Cutting into the neck, they dived
All night to the fish-swelled water

And flapped up with the catch lodged
In the throat, only to have

The fisher yank it out and toss
It gasping on a breathless heap.

Then to dive again, hunger
Churning in the craw, air just

Slipping by the throat-ring
To spray against the lungs.

And once more to be jerked back in
And have the fisher grab the spoil.

Men speak lightly of frustration,
And dim in the lantern light

The cormorant makes out the flash
Of fins and, just beyond,

The streamered boats of tourists
Rocking under *saké* fumes.

JACKAL

That he springs from a hole
And sniffs along the pit
For garbage delectable

Is no distinction: this any
Dog can do. And does. That
He flies at man-smell, canny

At hiding in places made
For roaches and the smallest
Mice, is not so very odd.

The sharp dividing line,
What makes us think of him
As neither out nor in,

Neither wild nor tractable
Is, first of all, his bark
Which is the laugh of a fool

Pulled out at midnight from
A reeking bed, and then
The outlaw look of him

As caught in the flashlight's shine,
Thin legs straddling something foul,
He yelps and bolts the town.

THE SQUIRREL

Gray fur to brown earth,
  The grasses clinging,
Eyes still bright, piercing

Through those topmost boughs
  Where, choked with nuts,
It clambered to the sun.

The rat has come to gnaw,
  The dog to sniff,
And I to meet my death:

Gray flesh to brown earth,
  The grasses clinging,
Eyes still bright, piercing

Through those tangled roots
  Where, crazed with fear,
I leapt from shade to shade.

THE LIBERATOR

Approaching the laboratory gate
He heard familiar squeals and, again,
Myriad rat's feet along maze-planks,
Then crows, yelps, mews: he was
Climbing the gangway of the Ark,
The Deluge boiling round his knees.

Entering, he glanced back where
The smashed glass door reflected head
And wobbly shins: the rest of him he
Must have left out in the drunken
Dark. Plucked on by cries of those he'd
Come to save, he passed frothed rows

Of test tubes, pickled embryos.
A swipe of the arm, and down they crashed,
Slicking the concrete floor. Still
The living urged him on: Out! Out!
It was a cry he'd learned to
Understand. When he reached the

Guinea pigs, unsnapped the toolbox
Lid and sheared the cage-wire, they licked,
All gratitude, the palm that
Offered crumbs. The rats, when sprung,
Scurried dizzily across the
Table strewn with cheese he'd cached

For weeks. And now, no longer
Running wild, the cocks, mongrels, cats
Fed beak by jowl together.
High above them on a stool, he
Smiled the smile of God, first
Work done, betrayals yet to come.

THE FINAL SLOPE

Climbing the final slope
He thought of them below
Ledged with the rancid goats.
   Two hundred feet to go,
Their envy snapping on the rope,

He spat into the sun.
Then the mountain threw him:
Like a butcher's beast he hung,
   Lashed to a crazy limb,
By pride and the wind undone.

By pride and the wind undone,
Legs swinging far beneath,
He felt the goats and their kids
   Nibbling at his feet,
And the sun's beak in his bone.

LIFEGUARD

All day they crush around his pedestal,
  Whiteness smoking on the bone,
    Lotioned fat

Of sacrifice. The sandgirls ogling up
  Like carp would shimmer gladly
    In his net.

You who lounge about them in this sweat,
  Enjoy while there is time what
    Soon must leap

To snare and snaring stay, to whelp across
  His strand a siege of castle
    Captains. Act

Before those waves, tall henchmen of his eyes,
  Cut in and drag the darlings
    To his arms.

41

AND THEY CALL THIS LIVING!

The sea that morning was as unruffled
As a tub of dirty water,
But we couldn't find the plug.
All right, we said, let it sit,
Let the gull keep dropping to the scum.

Then our son came running running
With one hand held up high. All right,
We said, let him dream a stained eyetooth
Right out of the Leviathan's jaw.
He's glad, and what have we got to lose?

And all right, we said, let the sun
Burn down at will. We'll furl
The striped umbrella and let it do
Its worst. For once, we said, accept
The ruddy show just as it's always been:

The sea as so much liquid having
No where else to go, an eyetooth
Some old peddler fished from a nosebag
As a relic to be bragged at school
And the sun the navel of us all.

Then just as sure as we were
Sprawling there, a wind sprang up
To knock the sea for loops
And spin the fishers in their smacks,
And the eyetooth started shrinking.

All right, we said, grabbing the kid
And unfurling the striped umbrella.
All right, all right as the sunburn started
Itching and we buried the eyetooth
In the sand—next time we'll know better.

SON

I no longer please him; he's found heroes
Whose exploits, of whatever style or magnitude,
Outstrip my own. Swinging a bat, running,
Shooting, you'd expect to be surpassed.

But it's also in the poems he reads,
Thoughts he cannot quite decipher.
Sometimes I hate what's dragged him
From my knees to lour before me,

Lofty with idols left and right,
Denying the castoff what shouldn't
Be denied a dog. Well, we grow, move off,
Despising all that's kept us from

Those misted vales and outlands
Roamed by dragons and redolent of maidens
Until, all heroes fallen,
We steal back home to clasp the only

Certain thing: which is no longer there.

I. M. JEAN COCTEAU

Who would bury
What did not
  Exist?

A puff of opium
Held over
  Seventy

Years between
The fat cheeks of
  Paris,

Your expiration
Dizzies and
  Bereaves.

PARIS

     With fifty thousand daubers
    To paint your face, you will never
Grow old, they say, with as many lovelies
    Legging up your squares, you will
Always gratify, they say, O with your river
      And your bridges and your quays,
    The mind need never wander to the north,
The east, the west, nor settle in the azured south,
     They say.

     Yet ask any two Frenchmen
    Spawned on the cobbles of whatever
Dreary *arrondissement,* ask them at the hour
    The terraces are emptied of their tables,
The chairs piled high, the sidewalks scoured,
     And looking to the north, the east,
    The west, finally to the brilliant
South, they'll say *Merde!* and *Merde!* again. That's what
     They say.

45

Ah, to one spawned on the asphalt
Of whatever American city, it is sweetest comfort
To know that, stripped of the décor, your gargoyles
    Pulled down (O hear the tourists sobbing in the choir!),
Bereft of the fifty thousand palettes and the
        Innumerable brushes that hide your face,
    You are no more ugly than that garish
Daughter who, after plying fabulously the Champs Elysées,
    They say,

        Ended up, five years later
    Under a gaslight in Les Halles. *Zut alors!*
I'd rather be a banker in Duluth, with a Swede
    Wife and two cars in the garage, than a
Boulevardier with ten *sous* in the pocket, a head gone
        Soft with dreaming north, east, west and south,
    And a kept bitch that cheers the porter in a
Greasy bed. *Mon Dieu! c'est triste la vie, n'est-ce pas?*
        They say.

AT VIRGIL'S TOMB

The bus stops just outside the gate
    Where all day long
The kids retrieve their soccer ball.

I watch and wait (in Ravenna
    Your Florentine
Lay starred on every tourist's map,

And gendarmes' pikes, like gladioli,
    Blazed around him).
Now as the tour-bus honks below

I imagine another Beatrice
    Entreating you,
In glory's dream, to guide her lover

Through that flaming labyrinth.
    At last you speak:
"Tell him to live remembering you,

Say that long ago man's boot ground through
    Inferno's crust,
The world he made, and will not know."

LINES ON AN 18TH C. TAPESTRY

It is a very pretty scene:
  As in a picture by Watteau,
The lovers seem about
  To strip themselves of all
Stiff finery and teach the faun

That stamps within the wood
  What violence a parcel
Of gallants bestirred, can wreak
  Upon a summer's greensward frail
With damsels of the blood.

On a damask stained with wine
  The ribboned marmosets devour
Such nibbled fruits and broken cakes
  That, envious in the wing-bright air,
The starlings cluster to complain.

His face uplifted to the sky,
  A lackey strums a mandolin,
But how should they attend harsh strings
  Who hear the song of flesh and bone
Stealing through their finery?

THE DREAM

He entered a zoo of reptiles
   Uncaged but chained,
Each with familiar face,
   Voice, claim on him.
The sunlight flashed off
   Scaly backs, earth
Clung to slimed jaws, the path wove
   Through and round them
From entrance to far wall—
   Dark, uneven.
But what most astonished as
   He passed the beasts
Was the cunning in the chains:
   Try as they might,
Muscles heaping, to claw beyond
   His shadow, which
Torn to strips of earth
   Was flung aside,
They could not. However single and
   Intense their claim,
However paws struck out, he passed
   Them unafraid:
Those chains rang solidly where they'd been
   Pegged in concrete.
His peace was like that of
   The tamer who,
After years of waltzing
   With the same cats,
Could lie for hours, head
   Between their fangs.

When he slipped the last of them,
    He came upon
A harem lined up in scale
    Of nakedness,
Faces like those one sees in
    Northern cities
Sharp at noon when shops and offices
    Debouch onto
The churning streets for sandwiches and
    Coffee. The first
Seemed very proper, and in one
    Or another
He recognized a classmate
    For whom he'd itched,
Head in arms, eyes swung back
    And climbing thighs
And into panties like sacks
    Of tropic fruit.
Yet unlike the reptiles these made no
    Move toward him.
They tried to win him
    With demureness,
Never mind as he strode on the ripped
    Skirts, blouses slashed
To midriffs. He knew them all,
    Just as they were,
With his lost fantastic eyes that were
    Always peering
Through and far beyond. And now it
    Was only fair

To pick one out and, he supposed,
  Save her from him
Whose chains would be the first to
  Give. Like a vain
Commander he went slowly by
  The lot, pinching
Here, patting there, then stood before
  The last of all,
Who posed, small hands raising
  Breasts, his mother's.
He rushed off, cheated, muttering,
  The smell so sharp
He must escape at once,
  And damn the lot.
At the wall the roaring
  Swelled where the beasts
Were strained and pawing at
  His back, the clang
Of chains like knells in
  A year of plague.
But the gate had disappeared.
  He groped along
The wall, which was horny to
  The touch and patched
With scales that formed
  Footholds, handgrips.
He leapt and slowly mounted,
  Fingers oozing,
Until at last he stared down at the
  Sea. The roaring
Ceased. He dived and woke to blackness.

VOGUE

Your women are judged beautiful:
Their underarms are hairless, legs
    And netherzones.

Clamped to their breasts are tiny
Rubber shields and, circling low,
    Those sheering walls

No arrow yet has pierced, only
Gold pulls down. Your women
    Go unrivaled:

Impenetrable as fortresses
They line those cold medieval streets
    No charger dares.

How you must weep to see them giving
Suck, your daughters, to dolls
    Of flesh and blood.

CHRIST OF PERSHING SQUARE

"I can prove it!" the madman cried
And clutched my wrist. "Feel where the nails
Went in! By God, I bear them still!"

Half amused, I shrugged and let him
Press the hand against his suture:
"All right," I said, "they cut you up."

Suddenly those fingers grasped
A hammer, it was I had hoisted
The cross his flung arms formed there.

"Yet," I whispered, "there remains
The final proof—forgiveness."
He spat into my face and fled.

This happened in Los Angeles
Six months ago. I see him still,
White blood streaming, risen from

Cancerous sheets to walk a Kingdom.

LAMENT FOR WELDON KEES

Could we have known that torrid night
A book of yours would sell
For eighteen dollars, we might

Have gotten a little drunker.
Weldon, where the blazes are you?
I can't help thinking of your

Wife, the lovely way she
Had of listening, holding her
Pride in you like a virginity.

We talked of poems, your "Robinson,"
And then you shuffled back
To slap some more paint down,

The canvas flat upon the table,
Under a light so fierce I thought
The paint would run. You didn't call

It that, but painting was your hackwork,
And surely the hope of poet's ease
Held you there from dark to dark,

54

The gin beside you on a stool.
I was green as grass, and you
My first live poet. What a bloody fool

You must have thought me! But it
Wasn't your praise I wanted then,
And thank Christ you knew that.

Just to be with you, and talk,
And drink your gin was what I'd
Come for. I left your room to walk

The city ragged, knowing at last
That poets were quite human.
Later, when I heard that you were lost,

Your car found parked too near the bridge,
I wondered which of us had left it there.
By then I too was hanging from the edge.

SOUTHERN TALE

From deep in the town the dancers' stomp
Will not rouse him now,
Where he hangs like a cracked bell:
Dark engulfs the man, the ashen cross.

The girl steps back and dreams—
O he the night and she the slippery moon,
And high the cotton flew!
It was like swimming in the river,
Water pressing to her deeps,
Ropes the arms that pulled her down,
The river banging on the wharf.

She looks away, her whiteness
Blending with the moon,
And hears the flies
Maddened by the smell of horse,
The smell of flesh.

From deep in the town the dancers' stomp
Will not rouse him now:
The arms, tongue,
Giant thighs are mute.

THE CANNERY

In summer this town is full of rebels
Come up from Tennessee to shell the peas.

And wetbacks roam the supermarts, making
A Tijuana of the drab main street.

The Swedes and Poles who work at Wurlitzer,
And can't stand music, are all dug in:

Doors are bolted, their pretty children warned,
Where they wait for the autumnal peace.

At night the cannery's like a train,
A runaway, cans flung up like clinkers.

Sometimes on an evening hot as Southland
When even fear won't keep the windows down,

One hears the drawl of Tennessee, the quick
Laugh of Mexico in the empty streets.

TO AN ASTRONAUT

Drink up! The night's a cave
Whose mouth, the moon,
Wastes to a hair's-breadth
Then is lost in clouds.

And who are you to climb
Such steeps of sky, where
Huge on hills of frozen
Light, the gods are ravening

And jealous angels, wakened
By your knocking, gather
Hailstones and the chunkiest
Pips of heaven to pelt

You as you rise? Already
Certain saints pray for you
In futurity, confused
By an image pierced

With the silver metals
Of its fall to martyrdom.
And those departed ones
Who shaped you lovingly

For this one terrible role
(And thereby entered Paradise)
Kneel in readiness
With wreaths and mute hosannas

At the icy tombstone
Each has wept for you.
Drink up! I say.
The gods roar, ravening.

SPEECH TO THE SHAPERS

They are wrong who think the end will be
Violent, rank alarmists who have
Visions of bombs bursting east and west
Together, leaving their hillocks of

Dead. Or who sniff already in the
Wind the poisons that will circle and
Devour. They have not lived enough who
See great armies joined along a strand

By nothing more than the bayonets
They'd stabbed into each other's innards,
With, to complete the savage picture,
Vultures and, moored with flesh, the buzzards.

And what must one really think of those
Who leap from Bibles reciting Doom,
When not only every Doom so far
Recited has failed, like rain, to come

But even the callowest Sunday
Schooler grins? The end will steal upon
Us as an average day, sometime between
Breakfast and lunch, while Father is down

At the office, Junior playing ball
And Mother is choosing lambchops at
The butcher's. Unannounced, it will drop
From a cloudless sky, or like a cut

In the power take us by surprise,
With all the lights snuffed out together.
But far more than the lights will go out,
And whatever's wrong will not appear

To be wrong, and it will have begun not
The day before, or now, or even
A thousand years ago. There's the rub.
We'll never know what hit us where, or when.

STEVE CRAWLEY

Why whenever they mention Hawaii
Do I think of you, and not the hula
Girls or orchids shrill against the blue?
Why when they send postcards of tourists tense
Around a burning pig, leis like collars
On a brace of hounds, do I see you flung
Across the earthfloor of that tent again,
Brains like macaroni puddled at the ear?

Steve Crawley, we found her letter crushed
Between the oilcan and the rosary
On your cot, and thought we understood,
But what puzzles still is this: what were you
Doing in that cathouse line, all brass
And itch, the night before the letter came?

THE PIT

Twenty years. I still remember
The sun-blown stench, and the pit
At least two hundred yards from
The cove we'd anchored guns in.
They were blasting at the mountains,
The beach was nearly ours.

The smell kept leaking back.
I thought of garbage cans
Behind chopsuey restaurants
Of home, strangely appealing on
A summer's night, meaning another
Kind of life. Which made the difference.

When the three of us, youngest in
The crew, were handed poles and told
To get the deadmen underground
Or join them, we saw it a sullen
Sort of lark. And lashed to trees,
The snipers had us dancing.

Ducks for those vultures in the boughs,
Poles poking through the powder-
Bitten grass, we zigzagged
Toward the pit as into
The arse of death, the wittiest
Of us said but did not laugh.

At last we reached it, half full
Of sand and crawling. We clamped
Nose, mouth, wrenched netted helmets
To the chin, yet poles probed forward
Surgically, touching for spots
The maggots had not jelled.

Somehow we got the deadmen under,
Along with empty lobster tins,
Bottles, gear and ammo. Somehow
We plugged the pit and slipped back
To the guns. Then for days
We had to helmet bathe downwind.

I stuck my pole, clean end high,
Behind the foxhole, a kind of
Towelpeg and a something more.
I'd stare it out through jungle haze,
And wonder. Ask anyone who
Saw it: nobody won that war.